HOPE IS A GOOD THING!

A Journey of
Healing and Growth
After Trauma and Adversity

DR. HOPE BEAVERS

Hope Is a Good Thing

PALMETTO
PUBLISHING
Charleston, SC
www.PalmettoPublishing.com

Copyright © 2024 by Hope Beavers

Paperback ISBN: 9798822967496

Foreword

When I first felt led to write this book, I laughed because my first response to God was that I don't even read books. I spent most of my life in school reading, so reading for pleasure was never really a thing. Honestly I wasn't a functional reader until about sixth grade, so reading was never enjoyable for me. The crazy thing is, I like to write. I have written my entire life. However, I know this must be God because He forever mixes my passions with my weaknesses. So this book is a walk of faith and me trusting His plan.

I have always felt that sharing our stories may help the next person. Our stories don't solely belong to us. My story may not be your story, and that's okay. However, hope is an element in every story. I pray my openness will open the door for you to feel safe enough to be vulnerable with yourself. Some of what you read or write may trigger memories you would rather avoid. Avoiding the memory doesn't make it go away. We must process and deal with those memories. That way, when they do come up, they will no longer trigger your trauma responses (flight, fight, freeze). The Pit Stops in this book are designed to help you process memories through various activities. The activities do not have to be done in one sitting and can be completed with someone you trust. Aside from the Pit Stops, you can also process these memories with a mental health professional if needed. Some people may also find it helpful to pray and meditate. Remember that hope has shown up for you thus far—allow the promise of hope to lead you further.

I hope you're ready to go on this journey with me. This journey is paved with transparency, vulnerability, accountability, honesty, and love. I can't promise you that this will be an easy journey, but I can promise you that it will be worth the trip. So before we begin, I pray that God will be the driver and you will be the passenger. May He dispatch His angels before you to prepare every stop to receive you. May your arrival be met with His glory. Most of all, may you heal and be elevated!

Table of Contents

Safety First

Hope is an intangible concept. As adults, we don't always believe that hope is even attached to us because we look at tangible things. But as children, we explored hope frequently. We did it through our imaginative play. Hope is the first thing we tap into when we want something and the first thing we give up when what we desire doesn't appear within our reach. However, we don't realize that hope is also living through God's promise: "For I know the plans I have for you," declares the Lord, "plans to prosper you and not to harm you, plans to give you hope and a future" (Jeremiah 29:11 NIV).

Hope is not only a promise, but a provision given by God. Jeremiah 1:5 (NIV) states that the Lord said, "Before I formed you in the womb I knew you, before you were born, I set you apart…"

The provision of hope was there when He set us apart. To be set apart is an indication of need and use (Romans 8:30). Otherwise, anything set aside would be thrown into the trash.

Think about it: we set things aside that we may need to fix or use later. Therefore, the idea that God Himself placed us aside should be mind-blowing!

However, if you are anything like me, hearing what God said to Jeremiah and applying it to your own life may be complicated. I used to puzzle at the fact that God knew me before He formed me, yet He created me anyway. Not that I am a terrible person, but to know me is to know all that I have gone through and all the pain it brought me. So the idea that God had plans to not harm me and to set me apart didn't add up. I even had a conversation with my husband about taking away people's trauma if we could. However, diving into this conversation more, I wondered who I would be without the traumas, challenges, and adversities I had experienced. Who would each person turn into without theirs? The answer is simple: I don't know.

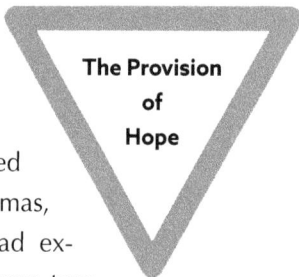

The Provision of Hope

I have always heard that God allows things for a reason. However, as I began to relearn God for myself, I realized that people were wrong. God did not simply "allow" trauma, challenges, and adversities to happen. Instead, God gave people free will, and sometimes people's free will interferes with our lives. So it's not that He saw something happening and turned away. Instead, God made a promise that "…all things work together for good to them that love God, to them who are the called according to his purpose" (Romans 8:28 KJV).

So God uses every adversity, trauma, and challenge for our good. Knowing this, I now see that for God to "know us," flaws and all, means that He had to give us provision (2 Peter 1:3) and a promise of hope.

PIT STOP

We don't often allow ourselves to talk about what we have gone through. Not because we don't want to, but sometimes because we don't see the point or have a "person." Write a letter to yourself about the things you have faced, particularly on any situation that plays on repeat in your mind. You can take breaks as needed. Do not go back and reread it. Leave it all on the pages unfiltered. We will come back to the letter later.

REFLECTION PAGE

Use this page to reflect on how the Pit Stop activity made you feel.

_____

_____

_____

_____

_____

_____

_____

_____

_____

_____

_____

_____

_____

_____

_____

_____

_____

Driving Me

I read in a book that we all have something that drives us. For me, it was fear—but not your ordinary fear. I'm referring to a *debilitating* fear. This fear started after the second time I lost everything. That time was significant because I had another life depending on me.

In the summer of my senior year in college, I started seeing a guy I met at work. He was kind and a single father. The way he showed up for his daughter made my heart smile. Now, I recognize that there were red flags.

I'm not going to lie; this relationship was not intended to go anywhere. I was in college in North Carolina, and he lived back home in DC. However, this summer fling changed my life. I became pregnant with my son while trying to get my birth control pills. I know you're probably thinking, "What about Plan B?" Oh, I tried. I was broke and could not manage to get fifty dollars to pay for the pill. Abortion was not an option. I'd done that once before (at sixteen) and vowed not to do it again.

Fast-forward: I'm in college and close to my due date. I had to decide to stay in NC and raise my son or go home so his father could be a part of his life. I'm not selfish; I opted to go home. Going home, I had nothing. My car was totaled a month or so before the move. I gave up my home and moved back with my mother. I went from two jobs to no jobs and had to get on public assistance. My sense of independence was gone. Oh, and to add insult to injury, my son's father opted out of parenting. However, I was prepared to parent on my own (kind of).

This situation was trau-matizing. People kept telling me it would get better. I knew it would, but I could not truly embrace this hope. Embracing hope during a self-inflicted trauma is difficult, especially when you feel like you deserve all the consequences that came from it. However, I have never been a fan of a pity party because I've always had something to prove. I remember asking my grandmother if she thought I would not finish college. She looked at me and said, "I know you're going to finish, if for no other reason than to prove everyone wrong." She was right. I was motivated by wanting to prove everyone wrong. I wish I could say I was embracing hope, but I wasn't. I wanted to show them I would still graduate college and be better than them.

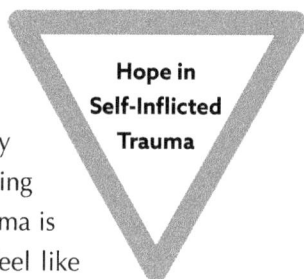

Hope in Self-Inflicted Trauma

This situation was terrible, and my attitude was horrible, but I sought help because my son's life depended on it. My mentor told me to pray. She said that sometimes the issue is not what you are doing, it's what you are *not* doing. So I prayed. I asked God to show me it all. I initially thought my pregnancy was the cause of my distress, but God showed me that my lack of humility was the cause. I had this superior attitude. I thought I was better than my family, and I looked down on them with harsh judgment. I let my desire to be better than where I came from turn into notions of being better than *who* I came from. My behaviors and way of thinking were out of order. God showed me that being better is not defined by material things or degrees but rather by a person's character. That shifted my thinking. I was no longer trying to be better than my family—I needed to be better *for* my family. I had to shift the generational trajectory. To do so, I needed to be humble.

Even with the positive outcomes of this situation, there were also adverse outcomes. I became fearful and anxious. I became a person who was scared to make big decisions. I also became afraid to embrace and celebrate my accomplishments. I thought that if I celebrated, I wasn't being humble, and that would result in me stumbling again. I believed any wrong decision could result in retribution. I developed a fear of losing everything. I hated this feeling, and it caused me to be frustrated with God. We have all been there, even though some of us are scared to admit it. I felt like I just wanted ed God to come out of heaven and say, "Go right, left, do this, do that!" If He did, I would be guaranteed an extraordinary life because I know how to follow directions.

However, that is not life. God is always with us and guiding us, but sometimes we can't acknowledge Him because we are focused on our fears and worries. Trauma, including self-inflicted trauma, produces fear. However, fear was never God's intended outcome (2 Timothy 1:7). God uses our situations to bring about positive change. God used my situation to show me humility.

Two times in the Bible, God says to be strong and courageous, not afraid, and not discouraged (Joshua 1:9 and Deuteronomy 31:8). In those same verses, He promises to be with us wherever we go. Both of these passages come from times of transition: the Israelites were transitioning to the Promised Land, and leadership was transitioning from Moses to Joshua. Like the Israelites, I was transitioning from one geographical location to another and from one leader to another. Many of us have found ourselves in multiple transitions. In these transitions, we—just like the Israelites—complain, question God and ourselves, and even think about going back. In the depths of transition, we don't embrace hope, even with the promise that things will improve. We are so busy focusing on what is happening around us and to us that we miss what is happening *for* us. Every transition has lessons that must be learned and things that must be done. The problem is, we want the prize but not the work. Everyone has to work to get results. Even the lottery winner has to leave home and play the numbers.

So one day, I challenged myself to go through a situation and not complain. Man, when I did that, I was able to see clearer. I could see what God tried to do for me during the transition. Then, I was indeed able to embrace hope (Philippians 2:14–15). I can't say I was no longer fearful, but I did not let fear drive me. I gained reverence instead of fear.

We are in a constant transition. To survive, we must allow ourselves to be led. Think of it this way: when driving somewhere for the first time, you need the navigation system to give you directions. We feel like we are in control, but really we are putting our transition in the hands of the navigation. Sometimes we try to take a route that we think is better. Come on, now—we have all thought we knew better than the navigation, which usually results in waiting for the navigation to reroute us. Either way, our transition is still in the hands of the navigation. We must realize that we need a leader to navigate us through life because we have no idea where we are going or how to get there. We tried it our way, but then had to go back to God so he could reroute us and provide directions. Just like the navigation system calculated the route with a starting location and the end location, God plans our lives (Jeremiah 29:11). So why is it that we are more likely to trust and hope in a manufactured device but not in the Being who knew us

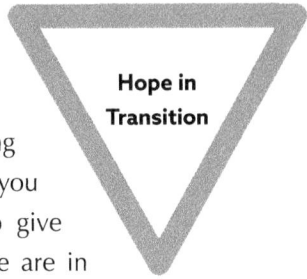

Hope in Transition

and mapped out our life before we were even formed? The navigation system can malfunction, and in those cases you are left to fend for yourself and rely on people to give you directions. If you are anything like me, you have checked out when someone gives you the second "make a right turn" direction. However, God told us multiple times that He is always with us. So no matter our route, we can depend on Him to lead us where we need to go.

So embrace hope over what's driving you. Embracing hope means having an optimistic, confident expectation of what God has promised. He said, "As the rain and snow come down from heaven, and do not return to it without watering the earth and making it bud and flourish so that it yields seed for the sewer and bread for the eater, so is my word that goes out from my mouth: It will not return to me empty, but will accomplish what I desire and achieve the purpose for which I sent it" (Isaiah 55: 10–11 NIV).

I don't know about you, but I will bet it all on God's plan working over mine.

PIT STOP

We've talked about traumas that were out of our control, but this section is focused on self-inflicted traumas and situations we put ourselves in. This chapter was one of accountability. Holding ourselves accountable for our actions takes work. It takes a level of complete honesty and self-awareness. In telling my story, I hope this gave you the strength to look in the mirror at your self-inflicted traumas and situations—not to relive them, but to acknowledge their part in your process. Fear is powerful, and it is a driving force for many. The good news is that fear can be overcome by embracing God's hope. In the first Pit Stop you wrote a letter. Continue to write the letter, but reflect and answer these questions:

1) Have I forgiven myself for the self-inflicted traumas?
2) Who or what is leading me through my current transition?
3) Am I focused on the promise or the distraction?
4) Am I complaining and stagnant, or learning and moving?

Hold on to the letter. We are not done!

REFLECTION PAGE

Use this page to reflect on how the Pit Stop activity made
you feel.

_____

_____

_____

_____

_____

_____

_____

_____

_____

_____

_____

_____

_____

_____

_____

Sightseeing

How do you hope when you feel overlooked?

In Fantasia's biopic movie, *Life Is Not a Fairy Tale*, there is a church scene in which she sings "Pass Me Not." I have heard this song many times, but the conviction in her voice made me receive the words. As the song lyrics state:

> "Savior, Savior. Hear my humble cry.
> While on others, Thou art calling
> Do not pass me by."

To know that God is calling others, you must first pay attention to their lives. Usually when we pay attention to the lives of others, we do so in comparison to our own lives. In keeping with transparency, I, like many of you, have lived my life in comparison. This behavior made me feel like I was not good enough. It even made me wonder if God saw or even cared about me. I have even asked God if He saw me and what I was going through.

I was taught that God sees all, but I felt overlooked. There was no way that God could witness all the trauma, bad decisions, and pain and not step in, right? Wrong. He *does* see us, and He does allow these things to go on because we have free will. That doesn't mean that He is passing us by. We look at other people's successes and wonder how they could get all they have, but not us. Well, the reality is that we don't know all that someone else had to go through to get what they have. We also don't know if God gave them what they have, since humans do have the ability to obtain outside of God. However, those things received outside Him will not last forever (Galatians 5:19–26).

When we're thinking about being overlooked, it's not that we are overlooked. Instead, we are not getting what we think we should have compared to those we are watching. In the same example used earlier, God had mapped out the plan for the Israelites to escape to enter the Promised Land. He gave them everything they needed. However, the Israelites complained and wondered if God saw what they were going through in the wilderness. They even compared their lives before leaving to their wilderness state. They did not trust God's plan because they were focused on their tough experience. If we are honest with ourselves when we feel overlooked, we ask God if He is sure. I have said, "Such and such has this, and they didn't have to suffer or go through x, y, z." I didn't realize that that person's x, y, and z were there, but I didn't see it.

Through all that I have experienced, I have learned that God is humble. He works behind the scenes. Just because we don't always see it, doesn't mean He is not working. Trusting in His plan is a recipe for hope. Romans 15:13 says, "May the God of hope fill you with all joy and peace as you trust in him, so that you may overflow with hope by the power of the Holy Spirit."

Remember, in the first section we found that hope is a gift, given when God sets us apart. This scripture tells us that we must trust God, and in return, we can overflow with hope. So it's not just enough that God gave us His hope; He tells us that we can overflow with it, too. We can have peace and joy in the process if we trust Him.

So God is not passing us. He sets us aside and steadily works on us to be what He has created us to be. We must trust the creator's blueprint and stop comparing ourselves to other models. You are custom made. The biggest issue is that you don't see yourself like God. You're looking through a veil. Veils hide you from others and distort your view. You have a distorted view of yourself, which comes from your distorted view of God (2 Corinthians 3:18). Your vision is blocked. That's why you can't see God, God's glory, the real lives of others, or yourself.

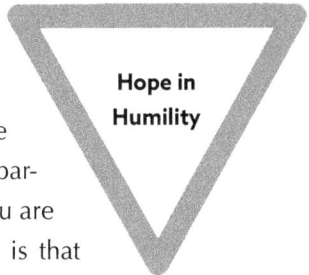

Hope in Humility

We are made in God's image (Genesis 1:26–28). If God foreknew you, He also predestined you to be conformed to the image of Jesus (Romans 8:29). In the first section, we talked about God foreknowing you and setting you aside, and that being set aside means you are of use. God set you aside because His plan included shaping you into the likeness of Jesus. Whew! That is heavy. To top it off, being predestined means that you are called, justified, and glorified (Romans 8:29). However, the prerequisite to be justified is to be unveiled. The veil is lifted through your choice to turn to Jesus. This justification comes from faith (in Jesus) and brings grace (through Jesus). The unveiling also represents revealed glory. It's important to note that glory is transitional. We move from glory to glory. So what you see now is not your finished image.

We celebrate this grace and glory. However, we're also required to celebrate tribulations. I know that sometimes it's hard to stop hiding because of the pain caused by tribulations. These struggles come as you transition. They bring suffering; suffering produces perseverance; perseverance, character; and character, hope (Romans 5:3). While hope is given to you, it is also cultivated through it all you endure. The hope produced from your suffering does not disappoint (Romans 5:5). What God starts, He will finish (Philippians 1:6). Hope is fulfilled (Luke 1:45).

Hence, God is not passing you by. He is shaping you. Keep your eyes on your journey, and you will see that the bumps in the road can't stop you from getting to your destination. Overflow in hope. Overflow in optimism and confidence. Move to your next glory!

PIT STOP

Take a moment to look in the mirror. Don't take your eyes off you. Look deep into your own eyes. Continue your letter and include the following: Do you like what you see? Not the outward appearance, but the internal. If you do, great! Write down everything you like and how to build on it. If you don't, write down what you don't like and the opposite of what you don't like. For example, when I looked into my eyes, I saw detachment. So I wrote down "detachment" and "attachment." I often feel like I don't want to attach to anyone in any way. So I wrote down that I want to have attachments with boundaries, safety, and love. This exercise may be uncomfortable because we are used to taking quick looks at ourselves, but we must look inward. Read Matthew 6:22–23. I hope you find the light in your eyes.

REFLECTION PAGE

Use this page to reflect on how the Pit Stop activity made you feel.

_____

_____

_____

_____

_____

_____

_____

_____

_____

_____

_____

_____

_____

_____

_____

Driving in Circles

Have you ever driven and come to a circle in the road with multiple exits? If you miss your exit, you have to go around again. For some of us, that circle or roundabout is the same problem that we keep running into. We keep missing the exit because we are not paying attention or there is a delay in the navigation. You will always miss your way out if you ignore the lesson that God is allowing you to learn.

However, the thing I like about the road circles is the multiple exits you can take. Each exists down a different path. So depending on the lesson you learn and your focus, you will take the right exit.

Furthermore, the key is learning the lesson. You can't repeat the same behaviors and expect a different result. You have to do something different. You have to keep your eyes focused and not on the distractions. You must stop waiting for the GPS to catch up and allow God to lead you. Understand that even if you can't hear Him, He will send messages along the way. You can't pass them by due to lack of familiarity or appearance. Think about it this way: if your GPS stops working and you have to pull over for directions, you are trusting strangers to give you directions. God will use whoever He sees fit to get you where He needs you to be. Often, we miss parts of this lesson because we want "help" to look a certain way or fit a particular criterion. Then we say, "I keep going through this mess, and God isn't helping me." The reality is He sent help, and you turned it away. The messengers came, and you dismissed them.

Also be mindful that others are in that circle with you, and that some are waiting to enter the circle to continue their journey. The thing about the people waiting is that they must yield to those who are in the circle before they can join. Some people buy into the generational curse ideology. But Galatians 3:13–14 (NLT) says, "But Christ has rescued us from the curse pronounced by the law. When he was hung on the cross, he took upon himself the curse for our wrongdoing. For it is written in the Scriptures, 'Cursed is everyone who is hung on a tree.' Through Christ Jesus, God has blessed the Gentiles with the same blessing he promised to Abraham so that we who are believers might receive the promised Holy Spirit through faith."

This means that Christ redeemed us (by our faith in Him). So if your family believes in Him and His works, then the curses are lifted. I would be remiss if I did not address intergenerational trauma. When our families don't resolve certain

things, we pass down our behaviors, mindsets, and emotions. Someone has to decide to
do something different.

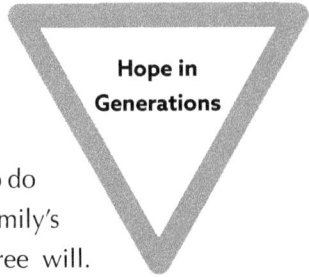

**Hope in
Generations**

Someone has to allow God to do
what He desires to shift the family's
direction. After all, we have free will.
That's what I love about God. He allowed
room for generational change and gave us the freedom to do
so. The next generations do not have to linger in the circle;
they can go to their exit immediately.

For me, that circle was a defining moment in my life. I
told you earlier that I lost everything twice from not being
humble, which allowed those who have seen me lose to
learn that humility is essential. It allowed me to teach my
children humility, so they can stay humble when they enter
their own circle of having what they perceive as everything.
Our stories don't belong solely to us. They are for us to share.

Furthermore, understand that those exits are hope. To
see ways out of the circle or problems means that there is
hope—a hope that says, "This problem doesn't have to last. I
can move on from the issue and no longer have to repeat this
lesson." Remember that hope is always with us, but we lose
sight of it when we focus on the problem, not the promise.
We can't embrace hope without embracing change.

Problems change us, but how that change happens is up
to us. We can let it change us positively by embracing the
lesson that God allows us to learn. Or we can let it change us

negatively and cause us to move about life angry, bitter, and hurt. Remember that emotional driving causes distractions, which usually result in accidents. However, if you drive intending to clear your mind, you are no longer focused on the problem but trying to find peace. Peace is where answers are (Genesis 41:16; Mark 4:39). Drive in peace so you don't miss your exit and won't have to revisit that same problem.

PIT STOP

In the next section of the letter, write out some of your problems. Then, review *only* this section to see if there are any patterns and themes. Once you do this, ask yourself what part you play in these. I'm sure you will see the lesson if you are honest with yourself.

REFLECTION PAGE

Use this page to reflect on how the Pit Stop activity made you feel.

_____

_____

_____

_____

_____

_____

_____

_____

_____

_____

_____

_____

_____

_____

_____

Passengers

I keep a small group of people in my life. I believe in quality friendships over many friendships. If I'm being honest, I do not trust easily, so it takes time to let people close to me.

However, when I do, I am all in. But like many people, I have not always made the best choices in friendships. Honestly I only learned how to be a real friend and receive true friendship in my adult life.

So what if I told you that some of the most disruptive people in your life served a purpose to get you to where you are and where you are going? Let me explain by calling this The JJ Experience. If you are a fan of classic shows, there is a show called *Good Times*. On this show, a character named JJ has a famous line: "dynamite." In the slang term that he was using, dynamite means something great. For example, "That dress is dynamite." However, dynamite, in its actual meaning, means an explosive device. Those disruptive people in your life participate in this double meaning. They are explosive… but also something good. I call this The JJ Experience not only because of the *Good Times* character, but because of two very infamous disruptive people, Jonah and Judas. They are prime examples of the good kind of disruptive people.

Hear me out! Judas walked with Jesus even though Jesus knew Judas had evil in him. Jesus called him a devil; he knew Judas would betray him yet allowed him to walk close to him. Jesus knew Judas' assignment. We have people in our lives that we know aren't good for us, yet we keep them around. We hold on to them because we see potential, and somewhere in us we like a good project. A lot of us have a savior complex. And if we're being honest, sometimes having these people around makes us feel better about ourselves. Just as we have our reasons, God has His reasons. These people are on assignment, just like Judas. They are on assignment to disrupt our lives to get us closer to our purpose. When you cut ties with these people, you usually learn a real lesson because of them. God also uses these people to show you that His word is absolute. He will prepare a table in front of your enemies (Psalm 23:5). So yes, they shake up your world…but they leave it in better condition than when they arrived. The good news is that these people will eliminate themselves and make room for someone better.

Now, let's talk about my guy, Jonah! Jonah wasn't trying to hurt anyone. He wasn't even a bad person. Jonah was simply trying to hide from God. He boarded a boat, and God caused the water to become turbulent. Jonah was even honest and confessed that it was happening because of him. He even told the men on the boat to throw him overboard. They pleaded with God to calm the water because they didn't want to throw Jonah into the water. Not because they valued his life, but because they did not want God to see them as murderers. Eventually they threw him over, and the water calmed down.

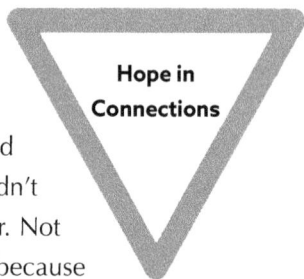

Hope in Connections

We all have a Jonah in our lives. They don't mean any harm, but they are causing a commotion in our lives. We justify keeping them around, saying we can't give up on them. The reality is that sometimes the longer we keep these people, the more confusion and chaos grows in our lives. One of the most valuable lessons I have ever learned was that everyone sent is not assigned. The Jonahs of our lives came to us but were not given to us. These are the people with whom boundaries are *not* optional—because the longer you hold on, the more your world is shaken, and like Jonah, they won't eliminate themselves. Let's face it: Jonah could have jumped.

One day, I prayed and asked God to remove every person in my life that He saw fit. I did not know that that would mean all my friends except maybe one. I felt alone. However, I had hope. I knew God would not leave me with no one. However, I also believed that God is restorative (Deuteronomy 30:3). We must have patience in suffering

(James 5:10) while waiting to be restored. Being alone may not feel like suffering to you, but at that point in my life, it felt like suffering. I already had abandonment issues and felt like I was no one's choice. So while I walked around like I didn't care, deep down, I did. Ultimately I didn't want to do life alone, even as I didn't want to fill space with people. However, hope is confident. It was in my hope that I believed that after a while, I would come out better (1 Peter 5:10). Besides, Job lost everything, but he endured and was rewarded in double.

Losing meaningful relationships when you have done nothing wrong can be challenging but necessary. Looking back, I celebrate my JJ experience because they disrupted and propelled me simultaneously. They made room for me to accept true friendship, taught me boundaries, helped me to believe people the first time they showed me who they were, and pray over every connection I have.

There's nothing worse than being on a long ride with a hitchhiker. I would rather ride with a friend. Who is in your passenger seat?

PIT STOP

Moving through life not knowing who to trust or build with is hard. However, pray over your friendships and connections. Be patient in your loneliness. In your letter, describe yourself as a friend. Then ask yourself what kind of people you are doing life with. Last, describe the friends or connections you desire.

REFLECTION PAGE

Use this page to reflect on how the Pit Stop activity made you feel.

On the Run

I remember being in my late teens, and my grandmother said I should stop running. Me being me, I asked her what she thought I was running from. In my head, I already knew. I thought, "I'm running from you all (my family)." She said she didn't know, but it was something. This question haunted me for a long time.

I knew I wasn't running from God because I needed him. However, over time, I realized I was trying to escape my hurt. You would think that my hurt would come from having been abandoned by my mother (several times) or having my father murdered in my home; while these things hurt, the most devastating pain was living with a preacher who tore me down and treated me like Cinderella. I was never emotionally abused or taken advantage of, but this living situation was significantly traumatic for me. It disrupted my very being because, until that time, I had been running my race; I was doing okay with managing my childhood adversities.

Eventually something broke in me. When I finally exited the preacher's house, I spiraled with a mask on. People around me thought I was doing so well. I never complained, vented, or even said much. I was giving "strong friend." Inside, I wanted to feel like I had control over myself and that I was someone's choice and not obligation. So when my grandmother commented about me "running" during this phase in my life, I felt stuck. I'm sure you have been asked that same question or something along those lines at some point.

Running sounds like a bad thing when we are asked that question. However, God called us into the race (Galatians 5:8), but what we do in it is up to us. While reading Galatians 5:7–9 (NIV), I had an "Aha" moment. The scripture states, "You were running a good race. Who cut in on you to keep you from obeying the truth? That kind of persuasion does not come from the one who calls you. A little yeast works through the whole batch of dough."

When I first read this, I would immediately answer, "The preacher cut in on me." It is so easy to put all the blame on her. However, it wasn't her. It was a cumulation of things that cut in on me. It was the preacher's unresolved trauma that she inflicted on me. It was the hurt that I experienced through intergenerational trauma, abandonment, loss, sexual abuse, neglect, instability, and being unprotected.

However, it was the preacher's behavior that broke me. It pushed me over the edge. We all have our breaking point, and we quickly blame it all on the straw that broke the camel's back. However, when we look at everything we have gone through, we realize that multiple things cut in on us and kept us from obeying the truth. We abandon the truth and start believing the lies our traumas and life situations told us. We become consumed by it. We become justified in our consumption. We live in a state of confusion and judgment. You may feel as though you're not consumed. It's okay if you believe that, but check in with your intrusive thoughts, day-dreams, sleep dreams, and emotional behaviors. Then ask yourself again.

In 1 Corinthians 9:25–26 (NLT), Apostle Paul says, "All athletes are disciplined in their training. They do it to win a prize that will fade away, but we do it for an eternal prize. So run with purpose in every step."

We run to receive control, safety, comfort, or stability as a prize; these rewards are good but not sustainable by our own hands. We run in the race but lose sight of the real prize. We train ourselves to survive but not to live. However, life is so much more than sur-vival, placing blame, and temporary fulfillment. We still feel like we are on an island. There's nothing worse than being surrounded by people and things and still feeling alone and abandoned. Our biggest problem is that we believe we are waiting on God, but God is waiting on us. "The Lord isn't being slow about his promise, as some think. No, He is be-ing patient for your sake. He does not want anyone to be destroyed but wants everyone to repent" (2 Peter 3:9 NLT).

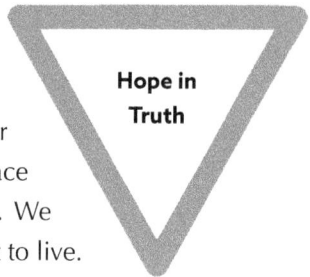

Hope in Truth

In repentance, there is truth and love. Love rejoices whenever the truth wins out. The truth always wins because God is the truth (John 14:6) and love (1 John 4:8). You are destined to finish the race because nothing has separated you from God's love (Romans 8:35–39). God's love never gives up or loses faith; it is always hopeful and endures through every circumstance (1 Corinthians 13:7).

At this point, you may be wondering how to finish this race. The answer is simple. Dwell in your truth. Whatever your truth may be, it's yours, and you belong to God. Your truth may be complicated, but it is comforting. Dwell in your truth without shame. We have all done things we are not proud of, but they brought us to this current moment. Also remember that hope does not put us to shame (Romans 5:5). Your feet may be tired, and that is okay. Your rest was factored in.

PIT STOP

We talked about blame, truth, and love in this section. Those are challenging to face. Continue your letter and include a list of all the people you blame for your hurt, traumas, choices, and other strong emotions. Don't reread it. Further instructions will be given later.

REFLECTION PAGE

Use this page to reflect on how the Pit Stop activity made you feel.

Rest Break

Have you ever taken a drive, and something in you told you to pull over or rest, but you just kept going, determined to reach your destination? I have. It has been the story of my life. Through my trauma, I have developed this "I have to make it" attitude, and it has caused me to fast-forward through life. Good memories are a blur or sometimes absent. People sit around reminiscing, and I can't recall the moment, but they told me I was there. I find myself in a constant state of exhaustion. The Lord says in Isaiah 28:12 (MSG), "This is the time and place to rest, to give rest to the weary. This is the place to lay down your burden. But they won't listen."

I felt convicted by that verse because I was a part of that "they." Sitting still in life has never been my thing. I have always had a "next"; I have always had something to accomplish. I came to a point where I sat in a stuck place. I had yet to learn what my "next" looked like. Sitting still took me to some dark places mentally, until one day when a friend told me I was in a season of breath. His words punched me in the chest because, for so long, I had been saying that I just wanted time to breathe. Yet God *was* giving me time to breathe, and I was over here complaining, thinking myself into a depression and going down a hole of doubt. Then I heard T. D. Jakes' sermon about being in limbo. That sermon helped me to see that I needed not only to breathe but also rest.

So here I was, not taking advantage of rest and breath. Here I was, not obeying or listening to God. I asked God to address me like a toddler, telling me step by step what to do, like in Isaiah 28:13. This is not okay, given that he had already progressed me from that state. Though His foundation in our lives has already been laid, something about being uncomfortable in an unfamiliar place causes us to want to retreat to ways or places of old. We need to remember why we moved on from those places. We forget the turmoil and intense emotions we felt in them, too.

Hope in Rest

Isaiah 30:15 (NLT) says, "In repentance and rest is your salvation, in quietness and trust is your strength, but you will have none of it." We won't have those things if we abandon the path that He put us on. We are quick to run from the unfamiliar and engage in self-sabotaging behaviors.

Embracing a new discomfort is not easy, but sometimes we make it more complicated than it has to be. There is hope

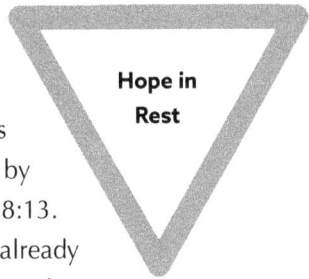

for us yet. Our hope is in God's graciousness and compassion (Isaiah 30:18). We must wait for God. We have to be patient and take advantage of the rest. God does not give or take you to new places before you are ready. He would not set you up for failure. Rest is not a punishment—rest is the next step in the journey. You will arrive at your purpose or destination on time because you rested. After all, it was a factor in God's plan. You are not in limbo; your next stop is not uncertain to God, but only to you. However, if we dwell in the resting place, he will renew our strength. Physically it is impossible to think clearly when you're exhausted. The next will become apparent when we listen; be steadfast and unmovable. Even in our rest, God is with us (Exodus 33:14). Rest is a part of the provision God gave you.

While rest is included, we only sometimes take advantage of it. For me, I felt robbed of rest. It wasn't an option because I couldn't turn my mind off. There is nothing worse than waking up tired; mental exhaustion is real. I told my husband that my exhaustion comes from the mental marathon I run in my head all day. That marathon includes replaying my trauma, a rehearsal of telling off people who hurt me, other peoples' problems, dreams of wealth, etc. You get the point. The crazy part is that we are not in a marathon alone. We just keep holding on to our traumas, problems, savior complexes, and survivors' guilt, but this marathon has a relay component that allows us to give the issues to God and let Him carry them the rest of the way.

However, this requires humility. It is essential to understand that through trauma, some of us develop hyper-independence, which makes us feel like we have to do it all and we can't trust anyone. So while your hyper-independence is justified, it is also misguided. God has never lied or disappointed us. His Word was always upfront and honest. We get disappointed and hurt when we perceive our wants and words as God's plan and words. 1 Peter 5:6–7 tells us to humble ourselves, and in due time, God will lift us and cast all our burdens and worriers on Him because he cares for us.

Humility is not easy when you think you are right, but it is necessary to be at rest. In humility, we present our traumas, other peoples' problems, and anything that disrupts our peace to God. In Mathew 11:28–29 (NIV), God says, "Come to me, all you who are weary and burdened, and I will give you rest. Take my yoke upon you and learn from me, for I am gentle and humble in heart, and you will find rest for your souls."

PIT STOP

During this section, we talked about rest. We also discussed being humble in order to get rest. However, I did not mention that a certain level of transparency and honesty is required in humility. On a new sheet of paper, write all the thoughts that keep your mind busy. Do not screen them; write them as they come to you. When you are done, take the list you have written and tear it up, put them in a helium balloon, and release it. As you let go physically, permit yourself to release it all mentally. After you release it, pray and rest.

REFLECTION PAGE

Use this page to reflect on how the Pit Stop activity made you feel.

_____

_____

_____

_____

_____

_____

_____

_____

_____

_____

_____

_____

_____

_____

_____

Mirror Check

Car mirrors are made to see what is behind and approaching you. It amazes me that we must check our mirrors every time we get into the car, as if someone adjusted them after the last time we checked.

However, I have noticed that there were times when my mirror shifted, and I had to readjust it. That is the story of many of our lives. We can't forget what is behind us because we feel like those things are never too far off. We are also used to looking at things a certain way and don't realize that we need to adjust our lenses.

I have moved forward from many things, but the emotional and mental impact of disappointment has always been in the rearview. When I accomplish a solo goal, I see it through and get the job done. However, when it comes to achieving a goal attached to others, that fear of disappointment approaches. I would create events for my business and personal life and cancel them out of nowhere. The thought of being disappointed made me put on the brakes. However, after the last event I canceled, I had to do a "mirror check" to see why disappointment was approaching me the way it was. I learned it was not approaching me to stay behind, but rather to pass me.

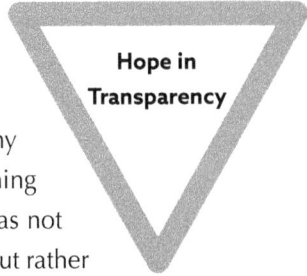

Hope in Transparency

As stated earlier, God promises that everything will work together for the good of those who love him and are called according to his purpose. I know that the events I put together are bigger than me and are meant to impact the lives of others. So I know these events are a part of my purpose and God's plan for my life. However, until I deal with my past disappointment, I can't carry out His plan. So when that disappointment becomes real, and when things get real, God shows up. I realized my disappointment masked my lack of trust in God's plan. While my disappointment was real, God said, "Girl, check my track record!" While others may have disappointed me, He has always shown up for me. I replaced my disappointment with trust when I took the opportunity to look in the visor mirror at *myself* and not in the rearview mirror at my past.

Someone said you can't drive looking through the rearview mirrors. I challenge that idea. You must look back sometimes, or you may not know what's approaching you or when to get into a different lane.

No matter what you see in that rearview mirror, you can move over and let it pass you. We have to allow our past to pass us to get in the lane God mapped out for us. We can't stay in one lane the entire journey. We must deal with, process, and determine when it's safe to move over and forward. Your past will always feel on your tail if you don't unmask it. There's nothing worse than driving when someone is riding your bumper. Every part of you (if you're like me) wants to slam on breaks to teach them a lesson, but you don't. Who wants to go through the hassle of the insurance and car repair process? However, avoiding the process takes away from the lessons we are supposed to learn. Now, I'm not saying slam on breaks and allow someone to run into the back of you. I'm saying move over and let that person pass because the lesson is not for them. It is for you. We must stop entertaining our past; rather, we must see it and process the risk of continuously entertaining it versus the benefits of moving forward from it.

In life, some things are always shifting, and mirror readjustment is necessary before reentering the journey.

PIT STOP

During this section, we discussed that sometimes, when we feel like we have moved on from our past, it creeps back up. Those things from our past can cause us to stop progressing or hinder our progress. What from your past keeps coming up for you? What is it masking? If possible, buy a cheap hand mirror and write the responses to those questions with markers. Then, if you desire not to see or experience those things anymore, pray that God helps you to move past them. Then shatter the mirror (safely, of course) and throw all the pieces in the outside trash.

REFLECTION PAGE

Use this page to reflect on how the Pit Stop activity made you feel.

_____

_____

_____

_____

_____

_____

_____

_____

_____

_____

_____

_____

_____

_____

_____

_____

Driver to Passenger

I used to find driving relaxing. I'm from DC but went to college in Fayetteville, NC. That was a five-hour drive. I enjoyed the drive. It was my time to listen to what I wanted and to be unbothered. Don't judge me: I used to be kind of petty. I never really told people when I was going home or anywhere, for that matter. My car was my alone time. However, after years of driving that ride and during my first career as a child welfare social worker (acting as an Uber driver at times), I was over driving. Now, I sign up to be the *passenger* for long drives. There is an exception to this. I usually drive myself if I'm going out because when I'm ready to go, I'm ready to go.

Relinquishing control to another person when it comes to driving is often straightforward. However, relinquishing control to allow someone to lead me has been a challenge. I was a person who needed to know where we were going and how we were getting there. I didn't do well with trusting others, especially when their lives looked like they didn't know what they were doing or after I had given them directions many times. It's giving: "How are you directing me if you can't lead yourself?" This mentality seems justified, but it's not right.

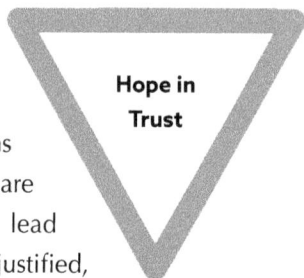

Hope in Trust

We often want help but reject it due to the way that someone lives their life or the choices they have made. Sometimes those are the people that God will use to drive you or give you directions. In the Bible, Rahab was a prostitute. She helped spies sent by Joshua to scout the land she was living in. Rahab hid them and later gave them directions on how to get back to Joshua safely; in exchange, they'd keep her and her family safe when the spies and their people returned. They made an oath with her:

"This oath you made us swear will not be binding on us unless, when we enter the land, you have tied this scarlet cord in the window through which you let us down, and unless you have brought your father and mother, your brothers and all your family into your house. If any of them go outside your house into the street, their blood will be on their own heads; we will not be responsible. As for those who are in the house with you, their blood will be on our heads if a hand is laid on them. But if you tell what we are doing, we will be released from the oath you made us swear" (Joshua 2:17–20 NIV).

I often wonder, if I was in Rahab's family, and she said to stay in her house and didn't tell me why, what would my response have been? In my judgmental phase, I would have probably looked out the window to see if there was a reason to stay inside because, in my head, I wouldn't have wanted to be in the house when her clients came knocking—you know, guilty by association. This thinking could have cost me my life. We look at people and make judgments and place limitations on them based on our own life choices, not realizing that we do not do everything "right" either. We also want help, but we get angry or frustrated and make ourselves believe that help doesn't exist for us. However, it's not that help doesn't exist for us; we just want help to look a certain way. We expect "*us*" out of others. But sometimes that unexpected helper who looks lost in the world can get you to where you are supposed to be.

I adopted the mentality of "if you can help me, help me." But like I said, I still have questions. There's nothing wrong with having questions, but sometimes we need to stop asking and wait for the directions to make sense. We want to relax but still struggle with trust. What if I told you we were designed to only partially trust people? Jeremiah 17:5 (NIV) says, "This is what the LORD says: 'Cursed is the one who trusts in man, who draws strength from mere flesh and whose heart turns away from the LORD.'" Likewise, Psalm 118:8 (KJV): "It is better to trust in the Lord than to put confidence in man." Or Psalm 146:3 (NIV): "Do not put your trust in princes, in human beings, who cannot save."

I struggled with my ability to trust people because I thought I had to do that. However, I realized I was not required to trust in people completely but in the God and the Holy Spirit that works in them. So we have to get to a place to know the Spirit *in* the person who offers help. God works through whomever He sees fit. He used Rahab to hide and give directions to the spies. Think about it: of all the houses they could go to, they went to hers. The house with traffic. (It never said they were serviced sexually.) They went to where they were led and didn't completely trust her. If they did, they wouldn't have made an oath with her. They were securing their safety by taking the oath. However, they trusted what led them to her and the Spirit working through her. They identified the God in her when she acknowledged the works of God that the spies and their people had experienced. She expressed her belief in their God.

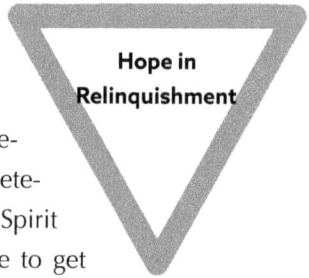

Hope in Relinquishment

So instead of feeding into the narrative that you must do everything yourself or no one can help you, remind yourself that help is an experience you put yourself in a position to receive. It is an experience that includes an encounter of trust and discernment. You allow your wisdom of people to align with the discernment of the Spirit to enable you to accept the direction and leadership. It's not easy, and it requires being able to table your intrusive thoughts, adversities, judgments, and traumas. It also takes accountability to admit that sometimes you yourself didn't and don't look like someone who should be healing or leading anyone.

PIT
STOP

In this section, we focused on our trust and judgment issues and their impact on our ability to receive help. Take a moment to continue writing your letter and reflect on some areas or situations where you needed help.
Ask yourself if there was guidance or support available. If so, what made you reject it? Also ask yourself what you need to feel safe enough to receive help. Lastly ask yourself if you are currently in a position to receive. Don't reread it.
Further instructions will be given later.

REFLECTION PAGE

Use this page to reflect on how the Pit Stop activity made you feel.

Rerouting

I love using the Waze driving navigation system. It reports real-time road closures and traffic. It will reroute you when needed.

Sometimes it can be frustrating because our current driving conditions are acceptable. Still, the navigation reroutes us for the upcoming traffic or road conditions we have yet to hit. I have even tried to stay the course despite being rerouted because I thought I knew best, only to find out why I was being rerouted later. We often find ourselves in this predicament in life. We stay in positions longer than we need to because we feel like it will lead us to where we are supposed to be. We dismiss everything telling us to leave.

I have learned that we are called to work, not positions. Our purpose is tied to the work that we do. Positions are milestones used to carry out our purpose. Positions are temporary. Think of it this way: positions are fluid. They change or end. If our purpose was tied to the position, where does your purpose lie when the position is no longer available or you're no longer needed in the same capacity?

This is often why people feel lost and without hope when they enter new positions in life or when their position changes. However, Proverbs 23:18 (NIV) tells us, "There is surely a future hope for you, and your hope will not be cut off."

The prerequisite of the future is hope. Hope puts us in a position to believe in the promise of a future. However, hope also moves throughout time if we believe. Our beliefs dictate how we move.

Someone once said, "Victims don't live to tell their stories, but survivors do." Living is one aspect that differentiates survivors and victims. However, *mindset* is the most defining difference between the two states. If I believe I am a survivor, I will move like a survivor. I will transition through life with the goal of living it to the fullest and leaving a positive impact while doing it. If I believe I am a victim, I will move through life going through the motions but maintaining stagnation. My position will not change. Therefore, my purpose will only be completed in part.

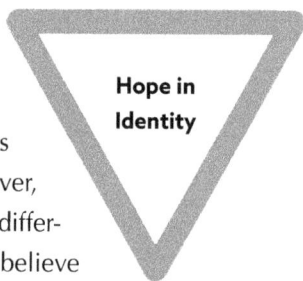

Hope in Identity

Survivors allow themselves to go through an unconscious growth process known as posttraumatic growth (PTG). Understand that trauma is not the sole experience in PTG; rather, PTG is an experience of positive change that occurs as a result of the struggle with highly challenging life crises (Tedeschi & Lawrence, 2004). Growth experienced is not a direct result of adversity but arises as a person struggles with the new reality following the adversity (Tedeschi & Calhoun, 2004). Therefore, the adversity itself does not promote growth; instead, the cognitive process utilized to acclimate, following adversity, is what promotes growth.

After a disruption to an individual's perception of the world and how they see themselves in it (also known as the "assumptive world"), they experience a process of rebuilding their core beliefs.

PTG signifies the evolvement of positive changes in an individual's self-perception, interpersonal relationships, and worldview after adversity (Steinberg et al., 2021; Tedeschi & Calhoun, 1996). PTG is an experience for people whose development has exceeded what was present prior to the adversity. PTG is a consequence of an attempt to psychologically survive and is often confused with resilience; however, they are distinct concepts. Resilience is often defined as the ability to continue with life following adversity and a return to *baseline* (Tedeschi & Calhoun, 2004). In contrast, PTG encompasses attributes of *change* in functioning (Tedeschi & Calhoun, 2004).

Therefore, the positions held before adversity, trauma, or challenges change for survivors. Survivors transition with new attributes that are useable for them and others. They experience the workings of the promise that "[all] things work together for good to them that love God, to them who are the called according to his purpose" (Romans 8:28 KJV).

Now, we are not going to count out the victims who are physically living but not moving forward. It is impossible to be the same person after your world has been rocked. But victims wear a mask of resilience to convince themselves and others that they are fine. They look as if they have bounced back and returned to normal functioning. They go through life without appearing to miss a beat. However, internally, they are struggling. They are fighting against the rerouting that would lead them to a new view and position in life. Anything new can be scary.

However, like any position, this victim state holds the potential for transition. Living victims can become survivors if they hope for it in faith and perseverance (Romans 8:23–25). Their transition is waiting for them to allow themselves to hope and believe in the purposeful life God promised. After all, God does not force us into anything, which is good, especially for people who have experienced trauma. Another forced event (even good) could do more harm.

Allow yourself to process what has transpired instead of holding on to what has happened.

The emotional distress will be there, but it could become less stressful over time. We must be willing to leave old positions and carry out our purpose in new spaces, with new lenses. If you feel stuck, ask yourself, What position are you operating from? Have you allowed yourself to be rerouted by God?

PIT STOP

This section discussed hope for our future as it deviates from a once-held position. Our beliefs and ability to shift perspectives are vital in our transitions. Please create an old-school map with each position you've held labeled with a yield or stop sign. The yields will have other positions on the road after them, and the stops will have nothing coming from them.

Compare your stops and your yields. In your letter, reflect on Whether your stops were by God's design, or were they your attempts to stay at baseline and "normal" functioning? Don't reread the letter. Further instructions will be given later.

REFLECTION PAGE

Use this page to reflect on how the Pit Stop activity made you feel.

AAA

I'm sure you know AAA, the roadside assistance company with all the discount perks. I love the idea of receiving support and reaping benefits from multiple sources. With AAA, even your family members can benefit from membership. While all this is awesome, we still recognize that one of the main components of joining AAA is needing roadside assistance, which includes being inconvenienced due to an auto issue. I don't know about you, but I don't like inconveniences. I have to get to where I'm going. I think it's the survival mode for me.

I was born in survival mode, literally. My mother was hemorrhaging, which resulted in an emergency C-section. The doctors informed my mother that I was not going to make it through the night. My aunt told my mother to

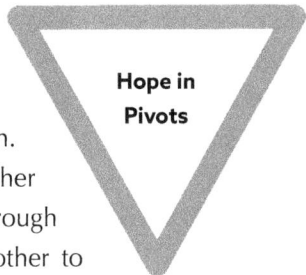

Hope in Pivots

name me Hope. In her mind, it was a "hope for today and a hope for tomorrow." What she didn't realize was that hope would define my very existence. Hope defining my life meant that everything about me looks like I can't, but somehow (by God and faith), I do.

Recently my current pastor, in his lesson, said we must change our minds. This concept was not foreign to me; I am a clinician. However, when he defined repentance's true meaning as a change of mind, it sparked something in me. All this time, I had thought repentance meant being remorseful and changing my behavior. I thought I was genuinely repentant. I had forgiven myself, asked for God's forgiveness, and changed some of my ways, but I had not completely changed my thinking around the issues that took up the most space in my mind, like finances and disappointment. We all have those themes that trigger us into anxiety or frustration. News flash: the enemy knows those anxieties, too. Those topics are the buttons that he presses on the most. Those are the areas where he plants doubt via questions. I was out of line in my way of thinking about these themes, but again, disappointment and financial problems were in my background. These background experiences caused me to get to many doors and stop; my struggles and tiredness made me decide to throw in the towel.

However, I adjusted my way of thinking through cognitive restructuring. I allowed myself to believe that God *got* me. I told God I trust Him because He never lets me down, and his track record speaks for itself in my life. So I stopped worrying about the money and the disappointment. I started to abide by the Holy Spirit's directives for the first time, even with uncertainty about my own abilities and other people's responses. I operated on the positive side of "maybe." I came into alignment. I stopped allowing myself to use faith and belief interchangeably because they are not the same. To *believe* something focuses on the ability ("this can happen"). *Faith* focuses on carrying out the ability (this will happen). Therefore, when we adjust our beliefs, it births our ability to tap into our faith truly. Thus, our faith starts with a shift in our beliefs and mind (John 11:25–26; Romans 10:9).

So while life throws inconveniences, we must tap into the other AAA experience…adjust, abide, and align. Adjustments to our thinking occur first (Romans 12:2). However, abiding and aligning are not done in a set order. Sometimes we dwell in alignment and then abide; sometimes we comply and come into agreement; for some, alignment and abiding happen simultaneously. Like AAA, your family (attachments) can benefit from using your AAA because our stories don't solely belong to us. Also perks that come with the AAA experience include peace, opportunity fulfillment, joy, boundaries, steadfast commitment, advancement, and more.

PIT STOP

This section focused on shifting our beliefs, coming into agreement, and abiding by God's Word. We all have those couple of themes that cause us to be uneasy, whether they're finances, relationships, or other challenges. I want you to track the reoccurring experiences (themes) that cause you uneasiness. In a day, tally how many themes or experiences come to mind. You can do this in the notes section of your phone. The next day, I want you to challenge those thoughts by saying the opposite of the thoughts or using encouraging statements whenever you have them. For example, I'm in the process of having to restart paying my student loans. At first, my thoughts were, "Every time I get comfortable, I go back to having to check my account with every purchase." Now I tell myself, "These loans will be paid, and I will be fine."

REFLECTION PAGE

Use this page to reflect on how the Pit Stop activity made you feel.

Parking

Have you ever pulled up to an event you weren't sure if you wanted to attend, and then found yourself sitting in the car? I have. While parked, we find ourselves deciding whether to go in or not. In those situations, I usually opt to go in. After all, I got dressed and drove there! Someone might ask why you would go somewhere you're not sure you want to be. While I don't accept all invitations, I believe that if I care about a person, I should show up for them however I can.

Sometimes we have to do things that we are unsure about. The journey you have taken through reading this book and completing the task was approached with uncertainty. However, you did it. You took on challenging tasks and processed or reprocessed traumas and adversity. Now, you have come to a point where you have to park and decide to operate in the freedom you have been given access to, or turn around and go back into old spaces. I'm not sure about you, but there's something about having to turn around that I don't like, especially the three-point turn. A three-point turn is a method of turning a vehicle around in a limited space by maneuvering forward and reversing multiple times to complete a 180-degree turn. It is usually done when making a U-turn is not available. After doing the work, God will not make a U-turn available. You'll have to maneuver through a tight area to turn around and return because you know too much now. You've changed. Your changes won't make it easy for you to fit into those spaces anymore.

So use the parking time to contemplate whether you want to operate in freedom. Freedom is a process and a choice. The good news is, you already started your process of freedom when you adjusted your thinking, believed, abided, and came into alignment with what God said to you and about you. These steps let you know the truth, which is the key to our freedom. Jesus said: "If you abide in my word, you are truly my disciples, and you will know the truth, and the truth will set you free" (John 8:31–32 ESV).

To know the truth is to know Jesus. Jesus said, "I am the way and the truth and the life" (John 14:6 NIV).

Hope in Choices

We have gotten to know Jesus through our human experiences. That is why God formed Jesus as a human. We needed someone to identify with. We needed to know that the being we followed *got* us and understood our experiences. He became every trauma and adversity that we encountered so that we could be free. He

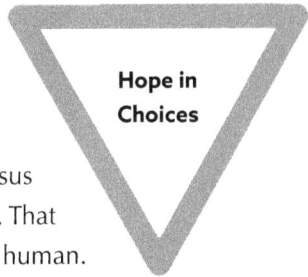

became our truth. Our adversity or traumas do not define our truth; our truth is defined by how we come out of them. "So if the Son sets you free, you will be free indeed" (John 8:36 NIV).

The doors are unlocked and open. All you have to do is decide to get out and walk into the best and never-ending event of your life: freedom. The choice is yours!

PIT
STOP

If you have chosen to move forward in freedom,
take the letter from the Pit Stop activities and seal
it in an envelope. You're going to mail the envelope.
There should be no return address, and your name
should *not* be on it. The receiver should be God.
It sounds ridiculous, but do it anyway. Wherever it
goes is where it should be, but most of all,
it is away from you.
If you're not ready to move forward, store the letter
in a safe space and mail it when you are ready. God
is patient!

REFLECTION PAGE

Use this page to reflect on how the Pit Stop activity made you feel.

_____

_____

_____

_____

_____

_____

_____

_____

_____

_____

_____

_____

_____

_____

_____

References

Steinberg, M. H., Bellet, B. W., McNally, R. J., & Boals, A. (2021). Resolving the paradox of posttraumatic growth and event centrality in trauma survivors. *Journal of traumatic stress*, 35(2), 434–445. https://doi.org/10.1002/jts.22754

Tedeschi, R. G., & Calhoun, L. G. (2004). Posttraumatic growth: Conceptual foundations and empirical evidence. *Psychological Inquiry*, 15(1), 1–18. https://doi.org/10.1207/s15327965pli1501_01

Tedeschi, R. G., Calhoun, L. G., Tedeschi, R. G., & Calhoun, L. G. (1996). Posttraumatic Growth Inventory. *Journal of Traumatic Stress*, 9(3), 455–471. https://doi.org/10.1007/BF02103658

About the Author

Dr. Hope Beavers is a licensed clinical social worker with over a decade of experience in her field. She leverages her extensive background to assist individuals, families, and organizations in navigating the healing journey from trauma and adversity. Dr. Hope is particularly passionate about supporting the "strong friend," advocating for those who continuously uplift others, believing they too should receive support. She is also the innovative founder of Elevating You, PLLC and Women of Elevation.

Raised in the culturally vibrant areas of Washington, D.C., and PG County, MD, her dedication to healing is deeply connected to her own life experiences and academic achievements. She holds a Ph.D. in Social Work from Walden University, a Master of Social Work from Howard University, and a Bachelor of Arts in Sociology from Fayetteville State University. Dr. Hope infuses her personal journey into her practice, fostering hope and empowerment in every interaction, both personal and professional.

www.ingramcontent.com/pod-product-compliance
Ingram Content Group UK Ltd.
Pitfield, Milton Keynes, MK11 3LW, UK
UKHW032220171224
452513UK00011B/671